SACRED PORTALS—
INVITATIONS TO COMMUNE WITH GOD

MARGARET MERLE

THY NAME
Publishing

Sacred Portals

Copyright © 2024 Margaret Merle

Publisher: Thy Name, Inc. (McLean, VA)

Cover Design: Maggie Dean
Website: Thy-Name.com
Contact: portals@thy-name.com

Rights and Permissions: All rights reserved. No portion of this book may be reproduced, stored in a retrieval system, or transmitted in any form or by any means — electronic, mechanical, photocopy, recording, scanning, or other — except for brief cited quotations in critical reviews or articles, without prior written permission of the publisher.

The Holy Bible Permissions:
All biblical passages from the NIV unless otherwise noted. Scripture quotations taken from The Holy Bible, New International Version® NIV® Copyright © 1973, 1978, 1984, 2011 by Biblica, Inc.™ Used by permission. All rights reserved worldwide.

ESV - PRINT - Scripture quotations from the ESV® Bible (The Holy Bible, English Standard Version®), copyright © 2001 by Crossway, a publishing ministry of Good News Publishers. Used by permission. All rights reserved.

ESV - E-BOOK - Scripture quotations from the ESV® Bible (The Holy Bible, English Standard Version®), copyright © 2001 by Crossway, a publishing ministry of Good News Publishers. Used by permission. All rights reserved. May not copy or download more than 500 consecutive verses of the ESV Bible or more than one half of any book of the ESV Bible.

ISBN: 978-1-7368128-2-2 (print)
ISBN: 978-1-7368128-3-9 (digital)

DEDICATION

Psalm 34:3
*Come, glorify the Lord with me;
let us exalt His name together.*

| Contents | Meditations |
| Invitations |

Before You Begin *1*
Miracles *5*
You Move Me *6*
The Turning *9*
See *11*
Moved by Delight *12*
And Let the Children Create *14*
Waiting *17*
Engineering Design Process *18*
Being in Want *20*
A Week of Meditations *22*
Poetry *31*
Creative Process *32*
Disorientation *34*
Something to Behold *36*
A Good Teacher *39*
A Prayer for Jealousy *40*
A Prayer for Envy *41*
A Poem When You Said to Write *42*
My Life Is but a Breath *44*
The Paradox of Significance *46*
Pace *49*
Liminal Space *50*
Fulfillment *53*
Musing *54*
The Night Watch *56*

Singing *58*
Sing Along *60*
Delight *63*
Battles *64*
Marriage *66*
A Prayer About Faithfulness *68*
Fixation *70*
Perplexity *72*
Desolation *74*
Dismantle *77*
Imagining What God Would Say About Pace *78*
A Study on Pace *80*
A Blessing for the Slow *83*
If He Asks *84*
The Gusting Wind *90*
A Story About Apricots *92*
Sitting With This Love *95*
Clean *96*
The Right Time *99*
Unquenchable Love *101*
Waiting on This Love *102*
Mercy *104*
Clarity *107*
The Far Away Stranger *108*
What You Aren't *111*
God, Listen to My Tears *114*
Unchangeable *115*
Making Fuchsia *116*
Discovery of Identity *119*
In Closing *121*

Before You Begin...

My hope is that these meditations provoke you toward sacred experiences that you will hold dear for a lifetime.

There are so many ways of experiencing God. If you read of the disciples who followed Jesus, or of the many saints throughout the ages who searched for the sacred, they all have wildly different personalities and experiences of the divine (much like you and me).

My hope for this book is that it will create opportunity to "be known as you are fully known." Opening up our heads, hearts, and bodies to more of God may just lead us into unexplored territory that we have yet to imagine. Cheers to your journey! Maybe you'll get to tell me about it one day...

Take these meditations and make them into whatever you want. Re-write them. Change the questions. Let them move you into YOUR territory. These poems are for you. Maybe a song or a Scripture will come to mind upon reading...move into those spaces. Be free!

The four main ingredients you'll find woven into each of these readings are worship, prayer, Scripture,

and invitations to experience fellowship. I believe these are the core ingredients of our sacred journey. I have gleaned from many wonderful sacred practices on my own sacred journey (Lectio Divina, The Emmanuel Moment, for example). While tools like these are widely known and used throughout church history by lots of Christians from various faith communities, I've adopted them here in these meditations to my liking (please adopt my work to yours!). While these ancient practices don't need improvement, I hope you'll see the freedom and creative license that's possible in our "play with God." Afterall, the Scripture says we must "become like children to enter the kingdom of heaven." Play on!

Miracles

Unfavorable odds
Time sped up
A gift given
Impossibility challenged
Momentum shifted
Helplessness met
Small as they are big
…glimpses of glory

Make a list of miracles either in your week or in your lifetime. There is no miracle too small for the list! Praise the Lord for each one. Make sure to choose one to tell someone else. "Ascribe to the Lord the glory due his name!" (Psalm 29:2 NIV)

You Move Me—

I'm frustrated,
Then find I'm in the right place at the right time.
I'm perplexed,
And find I'm on the same idea
You needed to be refreshed.
I'm fraught with a mixture of
Pressure and praise,
Only to find that it was all right,
According to Your perfect plan.
You moved me, positioned me, readied me—

Arranged things just so.
To the world it looked like a mistake,
But to You,
It looked like perfection taking shape.
Help me to see Your rhythms of
Divine grace over me,
Creating something vast
And intricately harmonious for
Your pleasure–
May it be mine too.

When was the last time you felt you were "in the right place at the right time?" Or maybe you showed up late to a meeting and, to your surprise, the "mistaken timing" actually blessed the other person...

How have you been "moved" by God this week? Search for His Holy Spirit in your memory...perhaps there was some way that He showed up and you didn't realize it was Him. Let's go back to the Scripture that says, "Ascribe to the Lord the glory due his name..." (Psalm 29:2). To me, this means that we give Him credit where it is due. Enjoy finding ways to give Him credit today!

The Turning—

Just when you think—
Just when you feel—
Just when you can't—
Just when it seems—
Just when it takes—
An illumination.
A resurgence.
A possibility.
A glimpse.
A yield.
The horizon.
          ...and then:

When have you experienced "breakthrough" in your life? Maybe there was an unexpected turning. Are you looking for breakthrough now? I invite you to dialogue with God in prayer about what comes up upon encountering this reading. I recommend listening to the song by Joshua Leventhal, "Lion | Lamb."

See
Seeds make gardens.
"Quick. Can you see it?
There's a shimmer there beyond the bank—
It beckons me to make light for a renewal."

What is beckoning you? What is the "shimmer" you're looking for? What strikes you about this poem? Does any Scripture come to mind? In prayer, you may want to ask the Lord to guide you to a Scripture to meditate on today.

Moved by Delight

What if we lived in a world in which everyone was moved by delight? How would this look?

What if life was a navigation into the waters of delight?

What if I moved with delight in the small decisions? In the large decisions? Where would I be headed? What would my body feel? My heart? My mind? I imagine honor—an unburdened people.

What if we saw this on a national level? On a global level?

Oh that I could claim delight in the things I have yet to know! I could be limitlessly delighted. The world's delight would be as limitless to me.

Where would I start? This brings me to the point—the goodness of limitedness.

Our limitedness shows us where to begin. It's the opening to a door which then invites us to collaborate with the delights of others. Our limitedness makes us a communal people.

A prayer to be moved by delight: *Connect us to our own hearts that we may know that we were created for the freedom of delight. Show us the goodness of our limitedness this day. Point us in the direction of where to collaborate with and to connect to the puzzle piece of someone else's delight.*

Psalm 37:4
Delight yourself in the Lord and he will give you the desires of your heart.

If we delight in the Lord, He may give us new desires or reshape desires we are already wrestling with. There may also be an invitation to trust your desires—afterall you are a worshiper! As you keep your eyes fixed on Him daily, through the power of the Holy Spirit, you can rest in the fact that your desires are good. This is not something you have to "work up." The Holy Spirit is faithful to do His part. He will use these desires in your life. I think about a piece of art being created. The artist had a desire in his mind as he began. Then, the final product: perhaps it is exactly what he desired, or perhaps it is nothing like it at all. The Scripture Zechariah 4:10 says, "Do not despise these small beginnings…"

And Let the Children Create

Creativity needs space, time, and freedom.
Ingenuity isn't timed. It isn't pressured. It
isn't tweaked until it's good and ready to
be asked. It's not pushed or prodded.

Creativity is birthed in its time. It grows.
It is praised. It is encouraged, then revised.
It breathes. It rests. It is fostered. It is noticed.
It is helped. It is reshaped.

When nurtured adequately, it isn't ashamed or
shy. When questions arise, it invites collaboration to continue to explore.

It reveals itself only when it knows it is ready—
then it's complete.

Creativity itself—just is. As God said, "Let
there be light," and there was.

It follows its creator's ideas. It follows its
creator's word.

It flows from the heart. It flows from itself.
It is. Just as "I AM."

Today, create something! Or do it sometime this week. You could ask the Lord to reveal Himself to you as you create. What do you hear? What do you see? Does anything strike you as "significant?" Perhaps there is something coming from a sacred place? Notice it. Absorb it. Cherish it.

Waiting

It's an art—a license of being a child. It's not hard. It's actually quite easy. It is the most simple of things. The lie is in the groaning—as if there was something required of you except to wait. When you submit to it—really give into it, it's like entering the easiest of lazy rivers. Going with the flow is all you ever wanted. Cheers to a year of going with the flow.

We live by every word from our Father in heaven and nothing more. If you find yourself "bored," don't worry— you're actually waiting. You were made to wait. You were made to watch. Don't forget the beauty in the simplicity of this life.

Don't fret suffering. Don't give into inaccurate illusions of suffering when the pain of waiting for the desired hope is all it is. Really, just wait. Give in to the movement of the Holy Spirit to stay put. You were made for this. Enjoy.

We are all waiting on something. Did this poem bring up anything new for you? If you feel led, ask the Holy Spirit to give you an idea that will "soften the blow" of the wait.

Psalm 130:5 (ESV)
I wait for the Lord, my soul waits, and in his word I put my hope...

Engineering Design Process

Engineers—Designers—People made for a process.

> What are you engineering?
>
> What are you designing?
>
> What is in process inside you?
>
> Around you? Before you? Behind you?
>
> In your hands?
>
> Perhaps there are things going undetected in the world right around you that are being engineered. Perhaps right in the very midst of you there is something being designed. Maybe something is forming right under the nose that is going undetected. Unnoticed. Under-observed.
>
> Right in the middle of things it can be unclear.
>
> What's the blueprint?
>
> What's the big picture?
>
> What's the goal?
>
> What's the vision?
>
> May there be space and the presence of mind to step back to see the big picture.

You are in process. Take the time to zoom out with God. Afterall, He sees the big picture. Scripture says that "...we have the mind of Christ" (1 Cor 2:16). You have access to His big picture if He will let you see. Scripture also says, "You do not have because you do not ask God" (James 4:2). Might as well ask! Perhaps you'd like to ask Him what His larger vision over your life is. What does it look like?

Being in Want

Some people call it "desire."

    Some people call it "poverty."

        Some say it's the place of being

            perfectly positioned to

                receive like a child.

Isn't perspective interesting? The same reality, observed from a different angle, could be the equivalent story, just told with something else in mind. When a piece of art is consumed by a group of human eyes, each person will walk away having received something completely unique. The same instructions given to a group of people, to complete the same project, may lead to wildly different creations.

Our need for God can create a myriad of human emotions. Being "needy" can evoke all kinds of desperate reactions. Yet, still, this is precisely the avenue to receptivity. To be in want is to be well positioned to encounter the majesty of God.

I invite you to go and look at a piece of art and ask the Holy Spirit questions while you look. Pay attention to what your heart says when seeing the selected piece of art you've chosen. He will speak. Wait for it. Believe.

Habakkuk 2:3

For the revelation awaits an appointed time; it speaks of the end and will not prove false. Though it linger, wait for it; it will certainly come and will not delay.

A Week of Meditations From Matthew 5:1-12

What is "blessing," really?

The word "blessing" has many uses—many connotations throughout history and in different cultural settings. The fifth chapter of the book of Matthew in the Scriptures has offered me an opportunity to peer a bit more deeply into the concept of blessing as it pertains to identity.

It is notable to me that, here, Jesus blesses individuals. He does not say, "Try to be pure." He blesses those that are pure. I may even venture to say, those that are already pure. This provides me with an invitation to wonder if Jesus may have seen something in us that we didn't see. Did he see some as pure, some as merciful, some with an innate ability to mourn?

This invites a lens to be taken to see those around us as already having these natural abilities. Jesus blesses each of these dear ones for a reason. What might this reason be? Could this be a way that all of us come into this world, carrying His very nature? Could it be that we all reflect him? That we actually are created in His very likeness—in His image?

We might delight and celebrate this likeness we share with Him. Afterall, Scripture tells us that we are made to be like the very God who did the creating.

At the same time, Jesus assures His audience that in the world they will be hated for this very likeness.

Is there a trait in this passage that reminds you of something deep inside you? Are there words here you have longed to hear? A place you have wanted to be loved? A place in you that has been yearning to be called "good?"

This place in you, this "trait:" has it been hated, maligned, mocked, persecuted, insulted, torn down, criticized—perhaps even by those who are meant to love you?

His "blessing" says that this very place, this way of being that reflects His nature in the world, is good. It's very good.

Read Matthew 5:1-12

You could ask the Holy Spirit to reveal to you if there is a particular piece of this blessing that He wants you to pay attention to for yourself. Then, find a new blessing on the consecutive pages that coordinates with what you hear.

Then, let this prayer be read over you:

I pray that, today, you will rest in your goodness. That you will feel the rest of His presence in all the areas you scandalously reflect Him. He honors you. As do I.

As Christ's body, together, let us start recognizing the beauty that we reflect. Let us resound His blessing by rejoicing over one another, His beloved, with loud singing.

Matthew 5: 1-12

Now when Jesus saw the crowds, he went up on a mountainside and sat down. His disciples came to him, and he began to teach them.
He said:
"Blessed are the poor in spirit,
 for theirs is the kingdom of heaven.
Blessed are those who mourn,
 for they will be comforted.
Blessed are the meek,
 for they will inherit the earth.
Blessed are those who hunger and thirst for righteousness,
 for they will be filled.
Blessed are the merciful,
 for they will be shown mercy.
Blessed are the pure in heart,
 for they will see God.
Blessed are the peacemakers,
 for they will be called children of God.
Blessed are those who are persecuted because of righteousness,
 for theirs is the kingdom of heaven.
Blessed are you when people insult you, persecute you and falsely say all kinds of evil against you because of me. Rejoice and be glad, because great is your reward in heaven, for in the same way they persecuted the prophets who were before you."

To "the poor in spirit:"
You who do not find yourselves enamored by what this world can offer—you open up the storehouses of heaven for the people in your life. You are in touch with your need for God and others. You make healthy relationships where neediness is not a place of poverty, but a place that creates the beauty of interdependence. Perhaps you've been belittled or feel the judgment of the world. To you, your reward will be great. The way you grieve the loss of this world and hope in a better future brings hope to all of us. Thank you for helping us know where to place our hope.

To "those who mourn:"
You are in touch with how to mourn. You make healthy mourning accessible to our communities. You experience the Comforter in a way maybe none of the rest of us do. You understand how sorrow and joy are interconnected. Maybe you are treated as though you're bringing the "mood down." Maybe you believe the lie that you are a pessimist. Don't forget the gift that you are to us. When you enter the room, you bring a depth that we desperately need. You understand intimacy the way the Father has planned for us to. Paul, in his second letter to the Corinthians puts it this way: "We always carry around in our body the death of Jesus, so that the life of Jesus may also be revealed in our body." Thank you for revealing Jesus to us. You bring the comfort of God and open up places of healing wherever you go.

To "the meek:"

You who do not need much praise or accolade: you wait well. The world may say you are lazy or not assertive enough. Humility is the posture that understands the servant leadership of Christ more than any other. Just dare to imagine your "inheritance!" Dare to imagine the inheritance you will give to those around you... I believe you open up dreams and make room for the power of God among us. You are serving Jesus when you serve us. When you choose to point to Him instead of yourself, you emulate John the Baptist's words: "He must become greater; I must become less" (John 3:30). We see you.

To "the peacemakers:"

The world may call you passive or conflict avoidant. Maybe you feel an ache in you as you see conflict all around you. Do you ever feel you attract the very thing that you are trying to avoid? I believe your presence "stirs the pot" at times because true peace needs to experience the complete process of reconciliation. The truth will be exposed by your presence. Whenever things start to look dicey around you, know that this too is an opportunity for peace. Where people have called you "placid" or "boring," remember that you bring the mighty hand of God to "make us lie down in green pastures" (Psalm 23). You carry the strength of a mighty rushing river! Be assured that the turmoil you feel could actually be the Holy Spirit working out peace all around us.

To "those who are persecuted because of righteousness:"

You who have been physically, mentally or emotionally abused by the world: remember that there is One who has and will fight for you. I believe the Holy Spirit in you will roar like a lion or be gentle as a dove at the right time. Do not let the world tell you that you are a victim—that because of how you've been treated, you are a failure. You are a king or queen! Own it. "He will make your righteous reward shine like the dawn, your vindication like the noonday sun" (Psalm 37:6).

To "those who hunger and thirst for righteousness:"

Do you constantly feel unsatisfied? Are you plagued by a drive to see things made right, while at times, everything feels wrong? Maybe you've even been discouraged from wanting to make the world a better place. Perhaps this insatiability towards righteousness eats away at you. Maybe you feel anger toward the world that tries to shut you down and shut you up. Remember that this craving in you is and will be fully satisfied. The now and not yet is already in motion. This process you feel so keenly is the working out of righteousness in a broken world. We need your drive. I believe you hold a key for us to create change from an empowered place of authority here and now. Point out the success of righteousness wherever you go. It's all around. The "not yet" has already begun.

To "the merciful:"

You who show us mercy: your compassion for others compels us to good works. Your fortitude to not give up in the most dire circumstances shows an aching world a kindness that we don't deserve. In the face of adversity, you bring strength to whole communities. You put action to the places where some of us see God's love as only an ideal that we feel could never be reached. Perhaps the world is trying to silence you or pour shame on you for caring too much. Maybe you believe that heaviness will overtake you. Perhaps there are lies surrounding you that you are critical and nothing is ever good enough for you. Remember that in you the Holy Spirit also places praise in the midst of the heaviness around you. You bring the healing balm of Christ practically to communities of people. Your "no" to evil makes space for the righteousness of Christ. You are incredibly strong and the enemy is afraid of you.

To "the pure of heart:"

You have been misunderstood and unseen in the world. Are you exhausted by people hoping to see you do wrong your whole life and you find yourself never caring to partake in their offerings? Perhaps people have left you because they think you are judging them? The truth is that others could be projecting the judgment they feel in their own souls when they are with you onto you. Do they need someone to blame when they fear that the truth will eat them up inside? This purity you carry will be missed completely by the world and you may feel that others are constantly questioning your motivations. They don't see your goodness the way you are able to see theirs. There is One who sees you. Remember that when you enter a room, people finally have the space to grapple with the righteousness of God. In your presence, people can't help but have a window to see themselves through God's eyes. Your vision to see the human heart the way God intended is incredible.

Be blessed.

Poetry

Beleaguering words musing on my mind.
    Art playing pictures in my head.
        Music dancing across my heart.
            Questions beckoning me further in.
              Language toiling in me still.
                Answers redeeming
                    that which we forgot.

Have you ever written poetry? Good thing is: there's no rules! Pick a Psalm to read. This is the BEST book of poetry ever written (in my opinion). Then, pen something down. It doesn't need to be eloquent. Write from your heart. Let if flow…

Creative Process

Watching my students has been a fascinating exploration of "creative process". It seems to me that when given a little space to "be" and to "play," a child's natural ability to create actually expresses itself with ease. They need no pressure to create. This process requires space, time, freedom, support, and safety.

Collaboration is key. No person in a team (however skilled or capable) seems to have "enough" without the others. They lean into one another for motivation, ingenuity, fresh ideas, pressure, pacing—to name just a few of the things they "borrow" from one another. Not to mention, perspective. Each sees uniquely. They need one another.

The word "and" seems particularly key for the harmony of a collaborative process. "Or" causes dichotomy and friction. Agreement, disagreement—each is vitally important to the tension and flow of the process.

The movement of the creative process is also fascinating to me. Sometimes it's slow. At times it's very fast. Other times, challenges seem insurmountable. It takes persistence and patience. To our surprise, it also requires rest—breath—reflection.

Creative process seems to house some element of suffering. In fact, Paul the Apostle made an interesting observation about suffering in Romans 5. He said that suffering produces perseverance, character, then hope. Perhaps being a "hope cultivator" requires a gauntlet of grit. I imagine that the grit simply births itself as part of the process.

John, one of the closest friends of Jesus, writes in 1 John chapter three that "hope purifies us."

However messy the creative process may feel, may you deem it significant. May whatever is being created inside you bring hope to you and to those around you.

In whatever you are creating, however small a thing, may you see the mystery and majesty of the grand possibility that may be housed within it for glory.

What are you creating?
Honor it.
He does.

Disorientation

It occurs to me that I find myself all bent out of shape sometimes. It is as if I even knew what "shape" truly was to me.

When I contemplate the idea of "orientation" (as if that were the goal anyhow), it seems I assume it comes from me. That really makes no sense at all upon inspection.

A compass points due north; a car simply goes the direction its driver supposes. Why should I be any different?

I claim that I am, "Clay in a potter's hands," but when I get down to it, I find that I must have actually believed at some point or another that the clay must mold itself—even instruct itself on what it must become!

I have a mind and am capable of reason—true. I have a heart that can discern its Maker—good. I have a body that can walk in this direction or that—indeed.

When I find myself disoriented, I must assume there is some point to the experience.

The clock can be reset, the stove readjusted to the necessary temperature—why, even the garden shovel put deeper into the earth still.

How am I any different? Is it really up to me to avoid all experiences of disorientation or can I accept it as a normative process for my "compass-self?"

Perhaps the true notion of orientation finds its origin at the point where God picks me up when I don't know which way is up and whispers in my ear, "Margaret, this is the way, walk in it."

Maybe I have no business judging the journey or even the destination that the Maker decides. I need only to rest in the knowledge of a Good Captain steering His ship for His good pleasure.

The Shepherd leads His sheep wherever He pleases—and that's that. It's good to be a sheep.

Is there anything disorienting you in life right now? If you feel led, write it out. You may want to inquire from God what His perspective is of this particular challenge. He will recalibrate you!

Something to Behold

Behold.

Beheld.
To be.
To hold.
To be held.

When a mother holds her child.
When a gardener checks the status of his carrots.
When a doctor discerns a plan forward.

To be pleased.
To check in.
To be vigilant of another.
To consume the presence of someone else within yourself— it's not full.

To consider.
To muse.
To ask.
To digest.
To taste.

A quest. It's only a quest. A never ending question with many-an-answer.

Behold.

Have you ever walked in a forest and felt it was far away? You wanted to reach out and touch it but it was beyond your reach?

Have you ever been with someone knowing they are far off and away? All you wanted to do was connect but somehow you knew they were not there? Out of reach?

I wonder what it will be to truly commune one day with God—with one another.
The Infinite One.
The Creator.
The One who stills wind and waves.

To behold Him for all that He is.

It's hard to imagine.
To be fully present to another.
To commune with a tree and actually feel its closeness instead of its vast distance.

I wonder how limited we truly are. Maybe the word "behold," in and of itself, speaks of a distance. Maybe it beckons us forward—to come closer. Ever closer. Maybe it's simply an infinite invitation.

To behold.

What are you regularly beholding? It could be fun to ask Jesus to put before you something He would like you to behold. What are you picturing? Don't evaluate it yet. Let your imagination flow. You can ask Him any question. What do you hope to know? Write down what you imagine He says. There is no "wrong" here...only play!

Isaiah 43:19 (ESV)

Behold, I am doing a new thing; now it springs forth, do you not perceive it?
I will make a way in the wilderness and rivers in the desert.

A Good Teacher

A good teacher doesn't "know."
They see.
They wonder.
They ask.
They quest, try, revise.
They inspire.
They encourage.
They guide and challenge,
collaborating in exploration "with."

I would wonder if all of us have teacher wounds to some degree? Maybe this led to some sort of "shut down" to a part of us developing. It's okay because Jesus IS THE Good Teacher. It could be cleansing to ask Him to wash away anything that a teacher spoke over you that was not aligned with His truth over your life. The Holy Spirit is more than able to do this. You may or may not feel anything as He works. He can even work in our sleep!

This Good Teacher honors you. He gives you ample time to work. He is not a task master. He is a cheerful collaborator and gives you plenty to do! He trusts you.

A Prayer for Jealousy:

When I feel locked out of my own story, reveal to me I already have access to what is mine. When I am discontent with where I am now, grant me contentment.

Show me what You are doing in my story now so I may live in the significance of the moment.

Give me trust that all You have prepared for me is already mine and Your goodness will continue to open doors to me when the time is ripe.

You are my eternal object above what You can do for me or give to me.

In You I have all I ever wanted.

Exploration of jealousy:
What does jealousy feel like to you? What would you add to this prayer for yourself? Are there Scriptures that come to your mind that you'd pair with this reading?

Something else:
Is there another emotion you'd like to write about? Fear? Anger?...

A Prayer for Envy:

Show me the goodness of my own story so I may not dwell on someone else's with wishing. May I long for the things that You have created me to long for and leave someone else's kind of longing to them.

Reveal to me the majesty You have prepared for me so I may stay focused on preparing to hold and steward the gifts You put in my hands.

Enable me to rejoice with those who receive what You prepared them to receive.

In You is fullness forevermore.

Exploration of envy:
What does evny feel like to you? What would you add to this prayer for yourself? Are there Scriptures that come to your mind that you'd pair with this reading?

Something else:
Is there another emotion you'd like to write about? Fear? Anger?...

A Poem
When You Said to Write

Write, You say.
Yes, okay.
What shall I write?

Write.
Wait, what?

Write.
Huh? Hm…Uh…

Go!
Where?

Go!
What?

Go!
Um…
Wait.
For what?

Get ready.
I'm ready.

Are you sure?
Yeah!

Are you sure?
Definitely.

You're not ready.
Get ready.
I am!
Wait.
Are YOU ready?

No.
Ohhhhh!!!

I'm not ready.
When will you be ready?

I'm ready.
For what?
Wait! What?
I thought you were ready?!

For what?
Prepare.
Be faithful.
Keep going.
For what?

Okay—you're listening.
Good.

I love how sometimes God speaks or reveals His heart, not so we will "follow correctly" but simply to get our attention because He wants to commune with us. Have you had an experience that didn't turn out the way you thought, but it turned your attention toward God? Perhaps that was the whole point!

2 Chronicles 16:9

For the eyes of the LORD range throughout the earth to strengthen those whose hearts are fully committed to him.

My Life Is but a Breath

If I vanished tomorrow—what of it? Would I be missed at all? Would this wee, little life bring any recollection at all?

Would it tell of Your mercy, Your goodness, Your love? Would it tell of Your sorrows turned joy? Your chains broken? Your eyes opened? Would it tell anything at all?

The secret things yet untold—cut short—not fully revealed—would it be significant at all? Would you have seen my love, felt my prayers, remembered a whispered promise of more?

My life is but a breath—wholly important—wholly insignificant. Dust creating beauty, resting in dust once more. Whatever You choose for lasting will last. My life is but a breath.

Who will remember the music sung? The poetry written? Photos taken—will anyone see what I saw?

Ah! Alas—there is One who saw what I saw, that heard my song, that listened to my thoughts from afar.

And we will sing forevermore…

This life sometimes feels like a vapor. How vulnerable! Does this poem bring up a piece of music you'd like to enjoy? In the last paragraph there are some "daily doings..." What would you put on this list for yourself rather than "music sung, poetry written, photos taken?" What in your life seems to go "unnoticed?" Take a few moments to realize just how "seen" these moments truly are by the Father, Son, and Holy Spirit.

The Paradox of Significance

How on earth can it be that the smallest of moments... the most minute of moments can hold such DEEP significance? Do I make this up for my own emotional amusement? If so, quite amusing. Well done! What is "true/solid/lasting" about these brief moments of seeming "significance?" We say things "hold" significance. Who is the "holder?" We imagine these moments have power. Like a domino effect, a lynch pin, a key, a starting note...

In the same breath, these small moments may actually be insignificant—of our own creation—delusional even!? Ha! They are opened and closed in a breath—a blink. As quick as they arrive, they are gone again! Does this briefness diminish these "significant" moments' significance? From dust we arise and to dust we return! Life spins madly on...and yet, at times it seems to stop—to wait. To stare. To hold importance for one...more...moment. And have you had the experience where a moment of significance, as such, lasted and lasted...and to others it was nothing at all!? Have you placed significance on things that others would throw away in an instant? Have you seen a mystery revealed that no one else could see? You notice the passers-by...rushing past. Not stopping to see, to share, to hold sacred what you have discovered. Perhaps you get to keep it!? Perhaps it will stay with you forever and ever!? Even though no one saw. It was just you. Only you.

Please, if this is true—do not let the naysayers, the non-seers, the passers-by inform your idea of what is significant...sacred. Hold it. Treasure it. Place it...somewhere. If only in yourself—if that's the only place you have.

One day you might just come to see that this treasure of yours was the seed that created a palace with many rooms for those non-seers to play in.

You may want to read this one a few times. What strikes you? Follow that trail…is there some solitary road you've been taking that might be creating a "place" for others?

Pace

Pace is perplexing.
It can be self-initiated, community-driven, or implemented by an authority. It is fast, slow, or medium. It can create steadiness, monotony, and comfort. Alternately, it can shift constantly, be thrilling, and perhaps a little craze-inducing.
Plug and play each of these options, implement the human heart, and I give you… FEELINGS!

RUSHED, BORED, FRUSTRATED, CONTROLLED, OPPRESSED, DELIGHTED, EXCITED, ENERGIZED, PRODUCTIVE, CONFUSED, TORMENTED…
the exhaustive list continues.

The only thing that ever works is entering into a loop hole…another dimension…I call it "timelessness." Be warned-it will make you late.

What comes up for you when you think about "pace?" Take this to prayer. Push through the hard bits. "Just ask the next right question" (whatever is the next is "right!").

Liminal Space

It didn't used to feel like this—going from one thing to the next—head down, trudging on through. Completing the day like a checklist.

Once the heart becomes open, it becomes rather sensitive in the liminal space—the space between. The heart needs recovery time from whom or what it has just encountered. It also needs preparation time. At times the phrase which seems best to describe the conundrum is: "whacked out" between spaces. Not knowing the next scene of life is already being engaged. The next scene is still completely unknown…but the heart and body know. They do know. The brain falls listlessly behind, panicking to catch up. There is no calendar. Only responsiveness to whatever life will bring next. This experience could even be described as being on "high alert."

Before real living began, boredom was the closest parallel to draw to this unique phenomenon. What to focus on next? Why no movement? No answers come. There are no directives from above…yet—no incoming text messages—no strong impulses to move—no action to take. So, wait. Wait for the wind to change.

While waiting, there might be perplexity, questioning, frustration, restlessness.

Resisting twaddle, frenzy, frivolity, or remedy—the waiting continues.

Surprise is found upon discovering the preciousness found here in the wait. Something is figured. Something is resolved. Something is prepared. Bandwidth is created. Strength rises. Rest is received.

Dare resentment be placed on the liminal space!

For this is where the capacity for LIFE is created inside. This is what the heart is open for—to be led. If there is no space for the wind to blow, flying is not an option.

Are there times in your life that have felt like "thresholds?" What "befores and afters" come to mind? What are places of transition for you that might be deemed "a waste." Look again. Ask Jesus to reveal the significance of this territory to you.

Fulfillment

Sometimes when I think about the idea of fulfillment I must be thinking of a product. Fulfillment isn't minimized to a single outcome. It is embedded deeply in each stitch of the garment it creates. It occurs in each shovel full of dirt it scoops as it digs its ditch. It's in each fragment imaged in a dream being dreamt. It is on each page of a story being told. Fulfillment cannot be stifled onto a last page but is delicately crafted into the bones of the life it is creating.

Jesus, show me where I have sequestered your fulfillments to one outcome. Show me the myriad of ways you have been fulfilling your plan for my life. Every day is a new birth. Every day there is pruning. Every day there is harvest. Help me see what You see.

Musing

Musing gets a bad rap around here.
Undervalued, under-scheduled, unconsidered, unseen, all-together disregarded.
Hard work is praised.
Production desired.
Results demanded.
Even in the creative arts, snobbery and convention have snuffed it right out.
They call it "planning," "crafting," "brainstorming" even—all to produce.
Pressured, diced, rushed, and skipped.
The art of musing seems to be all but lost.
You might even be wondering what it actually is…Why, no one may have even told you, here in this town!
It's actually quite productive, really.
Musing is mind play.
It's where dreaming meets dancing with no steps to learn.
It may be forgotten just after it has begun.
Oh, that's no matter—no one will ever know!
It's secret.
It's delight. It doesn't even need words, shape, form—and don't even begin to pair it with "result!"
The best things in life come from a good round of musing. If you don't get a good dose daily, you might need a doctor!
In a world where musing isn't embraced, it has to be secret.
But maybe it prefers itself that way.

Today, take a nice dose of musing! Express your ideas through writing, speaking out loud, or simply thinking to yourself or talking to a friend. Dream! Muse! Ideate! You are full of ideas. Waste a little time dreaming today. No results required!

The Night Watch

Prayers prayed into the night.
Unspoken prayers envisioned,
heard, or simply felt.
Awakened from a dream
with a deep sense of significance.
Suddenly or abruptly, called into battle.
Sitting as lookout over the dark.
Invited in a jolt into wonderful light.
Bringing warmth into the night.
Creating change.
Alternating reality.
Silent, yet powerful.
Unseen, unrecognized, unnoticed.
Would our world go on without it?

Have you ever woken up in the night and wondered if there was actually a reason? Other than hormones, anxiety, a dream etc.? What if there is something sacred happening? What if God just wants to steal a little time away with you in the watches of the night? Next time you find yourself waking up, praise the Lord in your spirit. Perhaps this is a "welcomed interruption."

If you're a parent of young children, I'll never forget the time I was having a lot of anxiety about how much sleep I was getting. I remember hearing the idea, "I'M IN CHARGE OF HOW MUCH SLEEP YOU GET." The idea that accompanied this was, "Wow, God is in control of ALL things and whatever He gives me will be all sufficient. If I don't get enough, He will provide something clever like an extra cup of coffee, a nap, or Holy Spirit, miraculous energy!"

He is ENOUGH.

Singing

"Out of the overflow of the heart, the mouth speaks" (Mark 4:23).

"Above all else, guard your heart, for it is the wellspring of life" (Proverbs 4:23).

From the inside out, it flows.
Bubbling up without intention, it goes.
From the sacred place to
the farthest shores…
Unknowingly, out of the blue, it calls.

Crafted and well thought out, it teaches.
Thought provoking mercy from it, comes.
Inspired and swiftly ushered out, it exhorts.
Comforting and caressing, it shepherds.
Guiding and directing, it leads.
Propelling into action, it serves.
All of this and more, it gives.

Are you a singer? If not, do you want to be?

John 15:7
Ask the Lord whatever you wish…

I had always wanted to be able to sing harmony. I thought it so beautiful, but I didn't have any musical training and couldn't hear it myself to pick it up naturally. Once, I was in the car and felt some boldness and possibility in asking God to give me a miraculous "gift of harmony." I'm not really sure why I thought that even possible—it must have been a "prompt of possiblity" from the Holy Spirit. Soon after, I began being able to hear it and practice it by myself. My own personal miracle! I mostly was in awe that God could open up the supernatural ability, desire, and drive to learn something like that.

Matthew 7:7
Ask and it will be given to you; seek and you will find; knock and the door will be opened to you.

Which line of the last paragraph of this poem strikes you? It was inspired by the gifts in Romans 12 (and a few others from Ephesians 4). Sit in Romans 12. You could ask the Holy Spirit to show you what gift you have. If you want to learn more about the gift, I loved Arthur Burke's teaching on what he calls, "The Redemptive Gifts."

Sing Along

When there's no song on your lips—sing along.
When you can't even form words—sing along.
When you don't know where to start—sing along.
When the night is dark—sing along.
When you're doing battle—sing along.
When things don't go your way—sing along.
When thoughts are maddening—sing along.
When you've had a bad dream—sing along.
When you feel awkward—sing along.
When you face anxiety—sing along.
When feelings are blinding—sing along.
When you feel nothing at all—sing along.
When you are intimidated—sing along.
Sing your way in—sing your way out.
Sing under—sing over.
Sing it through.
Sing for change.
Sing for movement.
Sing for grief.
Sing for pain.
Sing for joy.
Sing for yourself.
Sing for others.
Sing for honor.
Sing for freedom.
Just sing.
Sing!

Read this once more over yourself. Release yourself to sing today (maybe in the car or shower or on a walk)— sing for whatever reason you want to. Music changes us.

Delight

Where can we find delight?
Fascinating, isn't it?
We find it where we least expect!

We find it while worshiping.
We find it while making beauty.
We find it while sweating.
We find it in prayer.
We find it in suffering.
We find it in honesty.

We find it.

You say, "Seek."
Help me seek.
Bless You for granting, that I may find.
"Restore to me the joy of your salvation and give me a willing spirit, to sustain me" (Psalm 52:12).

Thank You for the simplicity of delight.
You have put eternity in our hearts.

Be delighted.

Here is delight again! Make a list of all the things delighting you today. If there aren't any—make some!

Battles

Heavy, overwhelming, burdensome war
Beat up, discouraged, war-torn

Invited in, to see another perspective…

A playground
Battle, raging
Pool-noodle swords
Glee
Laughter
Fun

"I the Lord have created the enemy to wreak havoc" (Isaiah 54:15).

What if we are all children at play,
acting out battle in the Maker's hand?

The war, already won
Every tear will dry
Every wound will be tended
Every scar, erased

Psalm 121:1-2
I look to the hills, where does my help come from? My help comes from the Lord, the Maker...

Once when I was feeling quite heavy, I imagined that the battle we were fighting here on earth was like kids playing in a park with pool noodle toys. To God, it was all play. If the Lord created the enemy to wreak havoc, that means THE WHOLE BATTLE is in the Lord's hand. I realize not all the battles FEEL like play. Come up into the Lord's hand and no matter how big your problem is, feel the Lord's mighty power there. Stay there as long as you'd like. What does it feel like? What do you see there? You could ask Him to show you how all of this is passing away. He can show you glimpses into life eternal.

Marriage

A gift given
A box opened
A dream realized
A deposit
An activation
A beginning
A promise
A covenant
A receiving
A listening
An engagement
An invitation to sow and grow
A challenge ushered
A sharpening
A crushing
A surrender, asked for
A re-shaping
An obeying
A whirlwind
A passion
Deep, unexpected love
Blood taken
An expectation
A reckoning
A reconciliation
A forgiveness
A wound mended
An adaptation
A forever begun
A dance on-going
A shallow pool
A deep well
A charge
A call to faithfulness & fidelity
A learning
A studying
A time to observe
A time to serve
Vulnerability
A following
A journey of faith,
trust,
and belief
A washing & renewal
A renaming
A groaning
A stretching
Gifts cultivated
An opportunity for empathy
A death
A resurrection
A dark night of the soul
A joy
A delight
Intimacy
A song
A war
A victory
A start
A forever
All propelled by love
Many waters cannot quench love.

Now in the eyes of another—propelled to become who I was meant to become.

God can teach about the concept of covenant inside or outside marriage. I wrote this when God was showing me about 1 Corinthians 13. Jesus is our bridegroom. This is true whether we are married or not. If He himself isn't our "eyes," as it says in the last paragraph, we may drown, whether we are satisfied in marriage or not.

HE IS ENOUGH to lift you wherever you are.

He can heal a broken marriage and a broken heart.

He can comfort you.

He can bring you contentment while you wait.

What speaks to you in this poem?
What challenges you?
Write down some specific prayers if you feel led.

A Prayer About Faithfulness

To the Covenant Keeping God:
To You, who keep Your own word to Yourself,
Praise be to You forever and ever.

You are with me when I wake and when I sleep.
You attune my attention and
Place it where it needs to be.
You are with me when I rise and when I fall.
You never leave or forsake me.

You are here—fully present.
You are engaged, alert and attentive to me.
You see the big picture.
You are safe.

You are infinitely good.
You have boundaries and say no when it's best.
The yes You create happens after you have said no.
My boundary lines have fallen in pleasant places.

You promise specific things.
You are alive.
You keep Your word.
You know me
And know exactly what the best plan of action is.
Surely I have a delightful inheritance.

I once woke up in the middle of the night with the phrase confronting me:

"I keep MY OWN covenant TO MYSELF."

In my life at the time, to me this meant: "I don't need your help to complete My promises to you. Stop striving." Hear this with every part of your being, He doesn't NEED our help to keep His word (although He might select it). This happened when God was making His covenant with Abraham. At the time, the cultural ceremony to make a covenant was for both parties to walk through a sacrifice as a symbol of promise they were making to each other. It was a "blood covenant" and two parties committing to keep their word to one another. God walked through His part of the agreement AND Abraham's part (Genesis 15). He is MORE than able. He knows and works with our inability. He can handle our weakness.

2 Corinthians 12:9
"My grace is sufficient for you, for my power is made perfect in weakness."

Fixation

Holes
Rabbit trails
Something that needs attention—finds its way up
Suddenly something brushed under the carpet
Roars its head
Is it a hole or a portal?
Is it a pest or a test?
Is this the pit or the bedrock?
Stewing or brewing?
Frustration or cultivation? Or both?
To fixate is to find
Just when you think you're stuck—
You find you are actually studying a barrier
Fixate long enough to find the crack
That will ensue a crumble
The rubble gives way for rising from ashes
Ash is a victor's call
Don't forget.

If you'd enjoy it, make a list of beautiful things that you've encountered today or this week. Meditate on those things. Let them fill your senses afresh. My Drivers Ed teacher used to tell me I'd go where I was looking.

Perplexity

Have you ever looked at something that you knew was objectively beautiful but you couldn't quite resonate with its beauty?
Or read something you knew was true but felt no connection to the idea?
When I hear the phrase, "Beauty is in the eye of the beholder," it reminds me of the words, "The eye is the lamp of the body, if your eye is healthy, your whole body will be filled with light" (Matthew 6:22).

Allow me this day to see what You see and illuminate the beauty right in front of me.

There are so many words we deem "bad." I remember a time when I was having a lot of shame while mentally fixating around a thing. I remember this freeing thought coming to me, seeming to say, "You're really focused...the sure deposit that you'll figure this thing out!"

Isn't God an amazing cheerleader? What is something you're focused on right now? I commend your focus and say that SURELY, the solution will be made clear to you soon.

Rest in the fact that God has given you everything you need for life and godliness.

You will find the crack.

2 Peter 1:3
> *His divine power has given us everything we need for a godly life through our knowledge of him who called us by his own glory and goodness.*

Desolation
But What About the Desolation?

Haven't You seen? Don't You care? Your solutions seem so arbitrary, so dismissive—not addressing what has been at all. In desolation You say to the widow, "Serve Elijah" (1 Kings 17:7-16). How does that address the lifetime of pain—asking her to go farther still—pushing her to the utter edge? How arbitrary! How inconsiderate!

But what we didn't see is that the miracle helps us forget the desolation. You don't "address" desolation, You utterly destroy it. As if it is no more—it is obliterated. As if there is no memory of it at all—the valley vanishes. It's as if it never was.

We ask for recompense, You give wondrous miracles

We ask for morsels, You give feasts.

We ask for payment, You give lifelong inheritance.

To the God of

"far beyond what we could ask for or imagine:"

May we not be held captive to the smallness of our imaginations. Break us out of the meager capacity we have created. May our imaginations be portals to the "far beyond," so we may tread on the heights where You are. Use the depths to carve out the "more" we were created to discover. May we not be so busy looking back toward fulfillment of small, fictitious expectations that we miss the majesty of what You are doing. Grant us, wholly, the ability to "forget" to "fulfill."

Dismantle

Take it down. Don't forget. This is GOOD. Unearthed.
Undone. A MESS. Disorder. Chaos that leads to rest.
He came to disrupt the ways of the world.
News flash: as do we.
Expect mess. Expect explosion. It is how it should be.

Not all creative processes are messy but I'd say, most are. If life feels a little undone right now, don't lose heart. Sometimes the mess proceeds the glory. One of the secrets of the sacred life is that there will be incredible loss and pain. It's all in God's hands. If you look, even briefly, at the Old Testament, God was willing to do ANYTHING for His purposes. He takes no prisoners. He WILL be glorified and make a way for us to have full communion with Him. Take heart.

Imagining What God Would Say About "Pace:"

Pace is a promise—a signal of what I AM doing.
Pace is a pleasure!

Just like the cool, summer breeze that intensifies—suddenly signaling a beach downpour.

Those enjoying "beachy" leisure jump up, excitedly running for cover (or deciding to simply play in the fun).

Take pleasure in the rain.

Take pleasure in the cool, summer breeze.

See beauty in the fog, snow, and all kinds of wonder-y weather.

The mystery of pace (like weather) invites personal preference.

But I KNOW when the earth needs rain;
I KNOW when to cancel events for "inclement weather;"
I KNOW when to bring rest to the earth and to your souls.

Even so, I realize when it is time to restore the sunshine.
Be careful not to let pace perplex, frustrate, or vex you.

Aren't I the God who gives you sleep and wakes you up whenever I please?

If you toil in the night, toil well.
If you slumber deeply, give praise.

All these things are a part of my divine cadence for you.

Enjoy the hard, easy, sad, happy—find delight in what I HAVE allowed.

You are in my hands—you're in my arms (and my heart).

Slow, fast, fumble-y, rushed, pushed, painstakingly turtle-like—it's all meant to be.

Wade in with wonder.
(And with praise—don't forget the praise).

Is there a rainstorm in your life right now you can learn to dance in? May the Holy Spirit help you dance. May He give you a word to encourage you right here.

Isaiah 61:1-3
The Spirit of the Sovereign LORD is on me, because the LORD has anointed me to proclaim good news to the poor. He has sent me to bind up the brokenhearted, to proclaim freedom for the captives and release from darkness for the prisoners, to proclaim the year of the LORD's favor and the day of vengeance of our God, to comfort all who mourn, and provide for those who grieve in Zion— to bestow on them a crown of beauty instead of ashes, the oil of joy instead of mourning, and a garment of praise instead of a spirit of despair. They will be called oaks of righteousness, a planting of the LORD for the display of his splendor.

A Study on Pace

I've been doing a personal, observational study on pace. It's been something I've wrestled with all my life. It's funny—even as a child, growing up visiting Oklahoma almost each summer, I'd return, understanding the frenzy of DC wasn't for me. I couldn't verbalize it then, but I knew I was a fish out of water, swimming upstream—fantasizing moving somewhere I could breathe.

As a teacher, it's been one of my great joys in the last few years to study my students' pace and give each of them the pace they crave. It was surprisingly easy to allow enough space in the room to let each child take the time they needed on their work. To eliminate competition was shockingly simple. Eliminating grades made space to observe them deeply and know more accutely how to help them grow.

Watching myself as an adult learner, I'm finding that on days when I give myself the gift of unlimited time, I go much slower than I ever realized—on chores, writing, thinking, prayers. Not rushing myself has felt awfully extravagant. I grossly underestimate how often I felt rushed as a child. I felt rushed by my family, teachers, classmates, and most of all, myself. All that time I was striving to compete with others' pace—to try and keep up—to try and fit in—to try and succeed, probably to be the best—to play by the rules of this town. Maybe I'm over-compensating in my extravagant slowness lately, making up for lost time...for the years of rushing or pace matching. I'll finally exclaim: it's a skill! It's definitely become a skill.

My mom used to describe me as a "slow, methodical learner." I never realized how pervasive that was in every area of life: with tasks, art, hobbies, relationships. I think I generally felt I was behind the curve in some way—so I sped up. Whirling on past life, hoping to keep up with the running speed.

With the high demands that chronically being rushed imposes on the body, mind and heart, I'm in recovery: pace recovery. This may be one of the reasons visiting Colorado makes me feel I can breathe. Fast isn't necessarily a high value priority there.

This might be why being an American at a Honduran wedding, where the bride was a cool hour late, made me smile. These are my people! Or whenever anyone is late to a meeting, it gives me great pleasure…it's almost an "ode to timelessness" whispering to me: "Ha! You can't keep up either. Me neither. It's okay. You and I, we can live outside of time for one moment when I say to you, 'It's okay, I really don't mind.'"

Of course anger, from the YEARS of striving to be on time places, flairs up in the same breath and I say to myself, "Maybe you…being late to our meeting… pin pricks the place in my soul where I've been working so hard (and succeeding) at being on time. But now you're late and 'how dare you' because I want to live in a world where I don't have to strive to meet my own demands of keeping up anymore: a world where it's okay to show up whenever you show up."

Remembering how I saw the taxi drivers in Spain all standing around hanging out midday… It gave me such pleasure to see their leisure. Their lack of productivity.

So, this is a plea for all the parents, teachers, coaches, youth leaders, neighbors of the slow and methodical: PLEASE, if you know a slower paced child—if God gives you the eyes to see their pace—give them the gift of time. It's a loving act you can give them. It communicates: "I love you enough to slow down my pace to let you go at yours. You are a good thing, just at the pace you were created to go. Don't strive. Just be."

I know how painful this will be for you rabbits. The turtles are dying out here in this town!

To any of you slower movers out there—
(You might not even recognize this about yourself because you've been trying to keep up for SO long):
Your pace is okay. It breathes peace, beauty and enjoyment into the rooms you enter. There is a "savoring" to your pace—a "completeness" to it. The "unhurried life" is what you can teach us. You have permission to go slow. I picture Jesus being unhurried everywhere He went, even though He was in such high demand. Everyone wanted a miracle, right then!

I'm so sorry you've been rushed, prodded, poked— deemed "bad" for this quality. Even though they don't see, know, or understand, there is value to your cadence. I'm so sorry for the way you have been enslaved to production, overstimulation, and consumerism. There are parts of the world and other cultures where you are celebrated, needed, and praised for the talents you have that unfold in the stillness of ample time.

So, do yourself a service: take a breath. Write a plea to yourself for permission for your pace. Maybe you don't achieve as much—but quality over quantity matters somewhere. Let it matter right here, in your current reality. Here is a hug for all you've endured. The shame, the mental barraging, the anxiety incurred: pour some love on all those old wounds. Be complete, sitting right here (maybe doing nothing). In some other realm time stands still. Thank you for providing a portal, a window, a vantage point for all of us to see "timelessness" right here.

A Blessing for the Slow:

I bless you to own your pace.

I bless you for all the ways
you've had to hustle up stream.

I bless you to crawl when others
demand you run.

I bless you to hug yourself for
all the times you were rushed.

I bless you to honor the
goodness of your cadence.

I bless you to move with
ease through this world.

I bless you to forgive the "pushers."

I bless you to rest in the
goodness of what your pace
brings (even if needing to practice
patience is a frustration to others).

I bless you to embrace love for
all the ways you bring the
blessed subtly of "slow."

"If He Asks" *is a piece that is a bit of an explanation about what it's been like for me to follow the Holy Spirit (sometimes…and then sometimes it's much different than this!). Since living life with the Holy Spirit, I have found myself doing many things…that surprise me: including writing poetry! I remember when someone first told me, "I think God wants you to write poetry." I would have said: "Um, ya RIGHT." Here, I only attempt to take a crack at what the mysterious process of following Him has looked like. Maybe it will prompt some thought for you about what your journey has looked like with Him...*

If He Asks

I won't do it.
No way.
Not in my
wildest dreams.
That's not my dream.
Never would I ever!
 Why would I put
myself through that?!

Exhausting
Taxing
Stretching
Uncomfortable
Scary
Shame-inducing
Exposing
Not interested!

What changed?

Finding myself in
new territory…
on new ground.
Nowhere familiar.
Nowhere planned.
A pilgrim.
A nomad.
Alone.
Sometimes.
Misunderstood.
Sometimes.
A traveler.

A wanderer.
Going…where?
Where are we going?!
What are we doing?!
What is the plan?!
Adventure.
Excursion.
Delight.
Experience.
Dependence.
LIFE.
Faaaar more exciting.
Unpredictable.
Risky, maybe.
Reckless, even?
Alive, though.

I have… questions!
Is there a guarantee
this will end up…
Good?
Successful?
A win?
Safe?
Profitable?
Fun?
Happy?
…Joy filled?…
ABUNDANT?
—At least.

What changed?
He got my attention.
I'm…following…

Perplexing
Interesting
Enticing
Invitations
Can't resist the question—
What if I…?

This is surprising!
I never wanted to…
I never thought I would…

What changed?
I'm listening.

I must!
I can't get away.
I'm compelled.
I'm drawn.
I can't get enough.

Every time…
I see You.
I hear You.
Wait…
Is that really You?

This IS You.
I can't deny it.
NOT what I expected but…
There You go,
proving Yourself again!
Showing off again.

This never gets old.

Is this real?
Is this a dream?
You're still HERE?
Don't leave!
This is painful but...
I'm alive.

You just can't
WRITE this stuff!

Slowly...
it's all changing.
And I'm left...
Craving more.
Watching.
Waiting.
Wanting.
Thrilled.
Hoping.
Just to see You once more.

Still...
Exhausting
Taxing
Stretching
Uncomfortable
Scary
Shame-inducing
Exposing
...perhaps.

But...Not interested?
— Oh, definitely interested!
What changed?

He captured my heart.

This is too much!
Don't.
Beware.
Careful!
This is crazy!
What are you doing?
Is it worth it?
Why are you doing this?
Why suffer?
Why pay the cost?
"…Why
what
when
where
how?…"

What changed?
He asked me to.

What has it looked like for you to experience the Holy Spirit of God?

Holy Spirit, come and pursue us afresh. Help us follow You, regardless of how hard it might be. It's harder without you. Thank You for the adventure it is in follwing You.

The Gusting Wind—

It chills me.

It disorients me.

It alters me.

It completely knocks me off my feet—puts me to bed.

It refreshed me.

It cleansed me.

It moved me.

It propelled me.

It compelled me.

It guided me.

It shall beckon me.

It shall call me.

It shall envelop me.

It shall cheer me.

It shall change me.

It shall redirect me.

It shall comfort me.

It shall give me hope.

It shall impart wisdom to me.

Always trusting that gusting wind blowing me here and there…

The last line of this poem is more of a declaration of what I "will" do.

Are there words in this poem that surprise you? If you do a little digging, the Holy Spirit does some surprising (and at times uncomfortable) things. You could take some time to ask the Holy Spirit to show you where He has been in your life that you deemed "evil, sin, or flesh." It might just change your perspective of the whole situation if you knew God was causing the discomfort. God isn't evil but, I've found, He's not paramountly concerned about human comfort.

A Story About Apricots...

Good ol' Trader Joe's. Life's simplest grocer. My local store was out of the finest apricot brand there ever was. To say I was troubled was an understatement. I tried to play it cool for a couple of shops but then I started to realize that apparently I did not appreciate a good thing until it was gone. The "Blenheim Variety Extra Choice/Choice Apricots" might be my favorite food item ever (other than strawberries). Choice INDEED.

Let me tell you. This is no ordinary apricot. They are perfectly tart and halved (so they aren't too thick)—taste just like candy! They make normal brands of apricots taste like imposters. Not to mention that they remind me of my favorite childhood pastry from Heidelberg Bakery (in case you're curious, it's still there... apricot hamentashen—what can I say? I was a child of specific taste).

So naturally, finding them just GONE, I sent TJs multiple emails hoping for a lifetime supply. Where, oh where have the days of classic customer service, sale schemes, and bribery gone?!

Then one day...one glorious day, to my surprise and delight, I happened upon them again. Not only were they BACK but there was a SECOND brand of almost the exact same tasting apricot on the shelf!

Moral of the story: often just when things seem to go awry to the naked eye, Someone behind the scenes is doubling the fun.

You could take this moral and use it to outline your own story. When has God been "doubling the fun" in your story when you had an assumption that things were going awry?

God, reveal to us where you are 'concealing to reveal' more joy and delight. Thank you for the ending you have in mind!

Sitting With This Love

The wildest of things.
To sit still with it.
To hold it.
To wait for it.
To be shaped by it.
Like taming the wildest of beasts—
Like having a pet tiger.
How does it make any sense?
Nonsensical, disturbing
Right down to the core.
The fiercest of things.
Making its home in me.

Does love ever feel "wild" in your life? Uncontrollable? Song of Songs 8:7 says: "Many waters cannot quench love." What power! If I'm honest, often my response to this kind of power is fear.

I like how the Scripture says it's okay to be a little afraid of the Lord. Thankfully, "The fear of the Lord is the beginning of wisdom" (Psalm 111:10). This kind of fear has a connotation of awe and reverence. The kind that says: "You could obliterate me if You wanted, but You won't because You're just too good."

If we are on the side of love, we aren't losing! Even if it doesn't end up the way we thought!

CLEAN

"You are already clean because of the word I have spoken to you" (John 15:3).

"We know that anyone born of God does not keep on sinning; the One who was born of God protects him, and the evil one cannot touch him" (1 John 5:18).

"Then I will sprinkle clean water on you, and you will be clean; I will cleanse you from all your filthiness and from all your idols. Moreover, I will give you a new heart and put a new spirit within you; and I will remove the heart of stone from your flesh and give you a heart of flesh. I will put My Spirit within you and cause you to walk in My statutes, and you will be careful to observe My ordinances. You will live in the land that I gave to your forefathers; so you will be My people, and I will be your God." (Ezekiel 36: 25-27, fulfilled by Jesus Christ).

Do we really believe this? What if it was true? What is "off" about us going on thinking of ourselves and others as "sinners?" How does our view change now, if we see each other in light of these sacred words? Jesus Himself said He wouldn't take us "out of the world." 1 John 5 also says that, "...the world is under the power of the evil one." So, the conclusion? Trouble will come.

Rather than point fingers at one another, may our conclusion of trouble be something more aligned with the words above. May we bless each other in our identity as restored, new creations. May we unite against our common enemy that comes to "kill, steal and destroy." May we have fresh strategies in the unity we have in Christ to face trouble as Jesus would desire us to.

How do we live aligned with these truths?

How would you look at your spouse differently because of these words?

How would you look at yourself? Your friends? Your co-workers? Your "enemies," who are really your brothers in Christ?

The Scripture says that, "...the truth will set you free" (John 8:32).

The next time we think that our brother is our enemy, may we look into ourselves, asking the Holy Spirit for the truth, so we may walk in glorious freedom. May we see what He sees.

Lord, our "bodies are clean—" wash our feet; wash our ears and eyes. May we see and hear as you do.

You may want to take some time to dig into this meditation. How would you answer the questions here?

The Right Time

It's the right time.
It's the right time for space and pace.
It's the right time for the right time.

It's the right time for acknowledgement of the truth
that beckons you from within.
It's right.
It's time.
It's the right time.

For pace. For Peace. For shalom.

When it's right, it's right.
Tell yourself it's time and it will be as you say.
The right time starts now and lasts forever.
It's the right time to be the right time.

Your way and your pace is good.
Calibrate to your time.
It's time.
It's time for things to feel timeless again.

(Remind me, remind myself! That it's right. It's alright.)

What would it look like to calibrate to "your time?"

Unquenchable Love

Will it overtake me?
Will it ruin me?
Will it require all I have?
Will it run the show?

Love never fails.
Love covers a multitude of sins.
We love because He first loved us.
Many waters cannot quench love.

Uncontrollable.
Unmanageable.
Unruly.

Righting all wrongs.
Healing all wounds.
Covering our shame.
Understanding beyond explanation.
Accepting us for who we actually are.
Revealing the truth of who we were meant to be.

Unbridled. Unyielding.
Relentless, reckless love.

It follows us all of our days.
It infuses us.
It envelopes us.
It propels, motivates, and stirs us.

What manner of love is this?
It is quiet, patient, gentle.
The strongest force I know.

Will it overtake me?
Looks like it already has.
May this love burn forever in, through, and to me.
Unending. Never-ceasing. Eternal love.

Respond in whatever way you may feel prompted to...

Waiting on This Love.

Wait for it. It will not prove false. It will not delay. The revelation awaits an appointed time.
Here I am again.
Wondering. Waiting. Groaning. Longing.
Here I am again.
Doubting. Yearning. Using my hands to cultivate something in the meantime. A bi-product.
Here I am again.
Being consumed. Being faithful.
Assuming it's productive. Assuming it's sacred. Assuming it's helping.
Watching. Feeling the eminence once more. It lurks around the corner. It stalks. It haunts.
Is it frivolous? Is it healthy? Is it wrong?
Is it to be counted on? Assurity: is it too much to ask?
If the strength alone is any cue, it's worth the wait.
It must be good. It must be sacred. It must be holy.
It must unfold graciously.
It cannot be rushed. It cannot be ruined.
Who on earth has been chosen to steward such a thing as THIS?!
One who is trustworthy. One who is capable, attentive, gentle, strong, kind.
This one is worth the wait.

Jesus is the bridegroom—He is WORTH the wait. When He comes, there is no denying it's Him. Although the wait is long, take heart! He has overcome the world! Waiting on the sacred plans of Jesus is the only option. His love, delivered to us in whatever avenues or time He chooses, is the best. It's the only love worth waiting for. It's the only love worth asking for. You may just see it in a glimpse of some other love you have, when you really look for His fingerprint...

Psalm 30:5b
...weeping may stay for the night, but rejoicing comes in the morning.

John 16:33
I have told you these things, so that in me you may have peace. In this world you will have trouble. But take heart! I have overcome the world.

Mercy—

The meaning of mercy, who could find!
Intangible, forsakable, far searching
of something "better."
The hidden glory, who could fathom?
Its meaning must be near
but a mirage seeming farther, farther still.
Once I thought it came close.
I could have touched it—
ungrabbable, unfathomable—
slip between my fingertips.
Unsearchable, unknowable.

And then—something spreadable, overflowing,
generous, cool came.
Ever increasing, indescribable—
overwhelmingly near.
From where and whence did it come—
I could hardly know?!
Bubbling, contagious, mysterious still.
Ever staying, ever keeping—radiant.
Inside out.
It's source tantalizing my senses still—
of where and whence did it come?
 I will be searching ever still.

What on earth is mercy? You're invited to begin a search and study on mercy if it beckons you. What is it? Where is it in your daily life? Begin this week to unfurl the layers of mercy.

James 2:12
   ...mercy triumphs over judgment.

Clarity

At first it's just disorientation.
Jolted into another perspective.
To see, to know, to circumspect.

Then the dust settles.
I ask. I receive. I hear.
The truth sets free.
The trouble dissipates.
The purpose rises.

"Just know. Just feel. This is for you.
Weigh in. Invest. Create."
And then. Clarity.

Rest is restored.
And we're onto the next.

What is your experience of "clarity?" You may want to journal about it to "see what you can see..."

The Far Away Stranger

The far away stranger. Always keeping watch. Waiting for her moment to become significant. She is waiting behind the curtain. For others to see. She is the main attraction but they have no idea.

She waits. She wonders. She practices her cue. Will the curtain ever lift or is this all pretend?

But wait! There's someone else there too! Someone who's been practicing as hard. Paying arduous attention to the stage directions too. I haven't seen him—well, not really. Just from a far. Could he be the one that's in the scene with me? The one who responds to my lines? Look at him pacing back there. So focused. We cross paths for functional reasons. He passes me a prop, gives me a smile. He comes over to bring someone water.

What's going on?! My heart is racing. I think the curtain's about to go up. Why do I feel like I'm mounting the hill on a roller coaster—about to lurch to the top? Anticipating the quick descent. All of the sudden, I see you there, in the chair next to me, as we make the climb out of the dark. You smirk at me—as if to say, "See, you knew I was here all the time."

The curtain opens. The first act begins.
We all play our parts. It has somehow all come together. The story makes perfect sense.

And the show must go on.

Do you ever feel like you are watching your life from a distance? Do you need to engage? Do you need to "step into your story" to be the protagonist? What is coming up for you upon reading this poem that you could pray into, journal over...set at our Lord's feet?

God, Listen to My Tears

God, listen to my tears
because words cannot express
the yearning inside me.

Unravel the feels
because they've spun me up,
whirled me around,
and I can't see up.

I know You're here,
attentive to me.
So listen to these tears
that I've been crying all my years.

Take action on my plea
that's loud inside me.
Put it to good use—

for this complexity

is a groan for my brethren

that sits inside me.

He hurts. He is hardened. He cannot pray.

He has no tears for himself.

So listen to my tears.

For you know what I mean when I tear them.

Listen to my tears

For I have to believe

they're productive in your kingdom,

even when they don't belong down here.

They're "too sensitive"

"too deep"

"too dramatic"

"too much for him and whom"

But for You, they are a perfect melody.

So listen to my tears.

Are there deep griefs you have been carrying?
Allow the Holy Spirit to come now to
"hover over the waters" of your life.
He sees.
He knows.
He has a plan for the future.

Psalm 23
> *Even though I walk through the valley of the shadow of death, I will fear no evil, for you are with me.*

Psalm 139:8-10
> *If I go up to the heavens, you are there; if I make my bed in the depths, you are there. If I rise on the wings of the dawn, if I settle on the far side of the sea, even there your hand will guide me, your right hand will hold me fast.*

Unchangeable

The flame is still here.
As strong as it once was.
The same. The exact same.
Each time, making me think
It will consume me.
Weeks become months.
Months become years.
Yet, it's still the same.
It's the exact same.
It is.
It truly is.

The Holy Spirit is amazing! His love is unchangeable. If you need a dose and "aren't feeling the flame," you can ask Him to fill you afresh. The pilot light just needs a little more heat. God promised the Israelites, "The Lord your God goes with you; he will never leave you nor forsake you" (Deuteronomy 31:6). Remember, just like in the picture of a marriage covenant, for instance, sometimes we "feel the flame" and sometimes we don't... doesn't mean that there's no fire!

What You Aren't

This isn't the color! No. I'm orange!
I'm a sunset. I'm warm. I'm hope.
I'm edgy. I'm cheer. I'm fun. I'm party.

> Funny. No. You don't get to decide.
> You are fuchsia .
> You are passion.
> You are intensity.
> You are soft.
> You are comfort.
> You ignite—but not like red.
> Like fuchsia.

No! I'm not.

> Funny. You can say you're not, but you are.
> There is no choice. This is what is.
> The choice is either to see, value, honor,
> settle, use, or own.
> But you ARE fuschia.
> Have fun!

What "color are you?" You can ask the Holy Spirit this question. Let Him speak to you in symbolism. Imagine what He would say to you. He cares about the details of our lives. Let Him speak to you in imagery, in senses, in pictures, in imaginary words…

Making ~~Fuschia~~ Fuchsia

I said I hated purple. You kept giving me purple gifts.
I said my favorite color was orange or red.
What was it?
You called me fuchsia. I couldn't even spell it.
You told me I was a fuchsia colored rose.
I didn't like it.

Then I remembered.
I could never quite describe my favorite
color as a child.
Was it salmon? Too pink. I went through a phase.
Was it orangey-red? I went through a shorter phase.
Was it burnt orange? I went through a phase.
Was it mauve? No. But I still tried to fake a phase.

I remember vaguely asking myself as a child if it was raspberry. Well, that was awfully close. Ironically, I never went through that phase. It was too close to home. It would have approached solving the mystery too soon. Then the game would have sort of…ended early!

Lavender was acceptable.

Maroon—acceptably mysterious.

Burgundy—acceptable.

Always mixtures.

No true purple.

No true orange.

No true red.

The mystery of the mixtures.

Then You said fuchsia—it is a flower housing true purple in its heart. Its outer edge is orangey-red with a hint of purple (for harmony)—nearly raspberry!

It was true always but here it is at long last—the mystery solved. I am two. I am three. I am a mixture of you and me and Him. I'm not alone. I am made from you and for You.

I am fuchsia. I am solitary. I am pure. I am harmony.
I am communal. I am social. I am me. I am him. I am
We. I am three. I am alone. I am with.
I am a mystery.

I am orange. I am red. I am purple. I am fuchsia.

In Discovery of True Identity—
enjoy speaking this prayer over yourself:

God, You are my True Father.
You have made me just so.
Show me who You've made me.
Show me how You adore—
the me that You thought up,
with these fits of frailty.
Allow me to see myself as You do—
Your perspective is just perfect.
It reframes anything in me that I would
see with lack—
with negation.
You honor me.
May I hear Your Voice over me,
honoring me.
So I may honor You
rightly.

In Closing—

*A final note of encouragement
from Magaret Merle*

A
deep
hope of
mine is that
you found
some freedom in
this read. Maybe
you picked up this
book when you had
the time or when you felt
the wind beckon you to its
pages. As a teacher, one of my
deepest pains is the shame that
sometimes readers find themselves
battling. There are many learning
styles and many ways of reading. I like
your way of reading. Thanks for reading
in your way. For reading free. May your
soul keep "delighting in the richest of fare"
and may you take courage in finding just the
way your unique soul delights to encounter words.

About the Author

Margaret Merle Dean has gone by Maggie since birth and uses her full name to remember her beloved great Aunt Barbara Merle, whom she was named after.

She has been working as a teacher for just shy of a decade. Some years ago she found herself avidly writing through an immersive prayer journey. These prayers seemed to have morphed into poetry, ever to her surprise. Her heart is for all the things she writes to evoke in others their own unique experience of God. She prays and believes that the Holy Spirit will continue to create beauty in her work for others and she's an avid believer that creative works give birth to new creative works. In reading her work, may you find yourself in the midst of making new creations as well.

Visit Maggie's website for current poetry:
Poetforpearls.com

Upcoming Book Releases:
Only Somewhere I Remember is a children's story.

She is also collaborating with fellow poet, Deborah Sun on a book of lament.

www.ingramcontent.com/pod-product-compliance
Lightning Source LLC
Chambersburg PA
CBHW061749070526
44585CB00025B/2843